The Scroll
of the Violin

Jim Bennett

Poems 4

The Scroll of the Violin

Poetry is about truth, yet this is a work of fiction in that names of places and characters are used purely for convenience. Any resemblance to actual persons, living or dead, events, or locales, is entirely coincidental.

Cover Image and design by Rory d'Eon

Cover photograph by Jim Bennett

Violin graciously loaned by MusicM

www.musicm.ca

Published by Lulu.com

ISBN 978-0-9881258-5-8

Acknowledgements

I owe a debt of gratitude to everyone who ever criticized or encouraged me. I would like particularly to thank the unknown IBM'er who, after *four interviews*, decided to take a chance and hire me *anyway*. I could not have had this life or lifestyle without that first leg up. I would like to remember Mrs. R. E. Purdy, who taught me in a special class for two years, and gave me permission to think, then demanded that I do so; and Miss M. Firth, who made my ability to remember (especially poetry, in Literature class) an asset in front of my peers. Sometimes being too quiet is, well, just too quiet. Somewhere in those years the decision to write, the realization that I was indeed going to be a poet, took form - sort of like an iceberg melting, but in reverse: big and indomitable.

I owe a lifelong debt to Richard Ketchum, who taught me that "the statute of limitations is crap," that I can do this.

A large debt will always be owed to my writers' group. Their steadfast criticism, encouragement, and support have been much appreciated.

In particular I would like to acknowledge the effort and insights of Sandra Aitken and Amy Corbin, who checked and commented on the entire volume.

I again thank MusicM for letting me photograph their violin, and Rory d'Eon for a neat cover image.

Finally I must thank my wife Patricia, whose support and encouragement have always been there, in tough moments as well as in the good times. We've travelled together in more senses than one.

Table of Contents

Table of Contents

Table of Contents

Unimaginable

it is too complex
to find the pattern of gusts in the wind
streaking rain in strokes across the beaver pond,
though we watch under whispering pines till the drizzle reaches us;
hissing with growing turbulence
as the branches bend, each singular pointed needle
is exactly drawn against the churning sky.
Do you believe the way God stirs the world
is exactly drawn against the churning sky,
as the branches bend, each singular pointed needle
hissing with growing turbulence?
though we watch under whispering pines till the drizzle reaches us,
streaking rain in strokes across the beaver pond,
to find the pattern of gusts in the wind -
it is too complex

Galapagos Search

Leaving the main ship
in our bobbing panga
I studied Your sky for revelations
beyond pelicans and veering frigatebirds
and saw garua mist the worn volcanoes

Crossing rough water
I searched the wake for Your stirring hand
and heard sentinel sea lions
barking while mothers called their pups to safety

When I walked along the fractured lava pavement
looking for Your footprints
I was startled by swift grey lizards
that darted from crevices

Hiking the guided trails I listened;
from the finches and tame mockingbirds,
and even the timid yellow warblers
in the cactus trees and thorn shrubs
there burst no song from Your voice

So I came last to the landing place
where the others huddled already against the chill
waiting the wave-tossed panga's arrival
late in afternoon that was streaked with thin string clouds
lit suddenly sunset crimson
as if Your blood
ran in veins across the dusk between earth and Heaven
while Your thudding heart
lifting the pounding boat by the bow
drove through the gathering twilight
to take us safely home

Dare I Believe

Dare I believe that Jesus bled,
that thousands from five loaves were fed,
that fishes found his net to die,
that God pronounced that fateful cry,
"forsaken", as flesh to be dead?

Two thousand years His actions said
come, follow Me, forget your head;
yet hear my mindful doubt reply,
Dare I believe?

I wake and work, break daily bread,
lie down and dream of Love's life led
the way He walked: am I to try
to live like that? Could God on high
accept this flesh? Whose blood was shed?
Dare I believe?

Greek Statue: The Goddess

Pure calm,
the changeless features carved in belief
in faces that watch the world forever;
only immortal sculptures share this grace
of peace above flesh, marble smooth beyond stone
's mere polishing of sweat

the cold blank stare of the statue moves us
to walk slowly round so as not to be looking
at the regular breasts and average figure
made more than normal by the waiting gaze
of the watching goddess

Caught by the hand of the careful craftsman
in steady awe of his very subject
long dead and still disturbing execution
of inhuman poise
in impersonal blind eyes

Worn Dream

nylons under a woolen dress
swish hissing sleek electricity
curved seams reaching from slender heels
toward hidden hips under swaying pleats
    a worn dream is like an old radio drama
    images conjured through crackling static
    words plots confused a Prokovief tale
    now a leitmotif stirs for our longing hero
        and summons his found or lost heroine
    waking to nightmare nights in a dank apartment
    unclutching sleep hands stiff to switch
    the light in a fumble from pillow to washstand
    shuffling slippers drown tap-dripping echoes
triumphant, recalled, throbs the heroine's come-back theme
blood pounding brains warming up like an antique radio
pulse hissing pure electricity
remembering anticipating
    feeling sheer nylon flesh under woolen skirts

Annunciation

GOD wishes to announce
the following changes effective immediately:

    - the weather alters by accident
    - each sparrow flies or falls on its own
    - the value of Xmas is in merchandising
    - Sundays are free for rest or whatever
    - ask a Scientist to explain everything.
I quit.
 Amen.

To Sleep

Death sings

   but few heroes;

to bored gods death drones on

   chanting the list of normal names

to sleep

TakeBack

Good God

take back pleasing

some of Thy people all

of their time and surprise every

one once

Of Skies and Boundaries

beyond

disagreement

of skies and boundaries

expounded by the word of man

is god

Oracle

the Gods once spoke
aloud to all the world

through rough cliff's shrugging shoulders
in cave mouth's breathing shadows
moaning shapes in a charging sea

and in treacherous places
through quirk of rock and echo, mindful words
made us Oracles

Just

It's just a rented bus, a jalopy
lurching a broken road from the Ingushetia
border to Grozny
screeched to a stop in a cloud of diesel fumes

Listen and search the rubble
it's just a cellar full of dog-cornered children
sharing unclean water and straw for food

Load them up get moving
Looking back in the cracked side mirror
it's just a landscape of fallen business towers
smashed apartments flattened houses
and splintered trees
with smoke suggesting mined fields

and the coming roar
is just a helicopter surveying
please God let it pass us go shoot elsewhere

how can the manufacturers of war
explosive missiles, incendiary devices
and cluster bombs, how can the soaring pilots
with their launchers, how can armour plate battalions
with clanking tanktreads crushing

explain to shell-stunned starving refugees
with all the patience of mute children
how their leaders assure them, telling all the world
that this devastation

of their cause
is just

Agnostic II

without

God's confession

      agnostic denial

faith is a fact some have to live

      without

Dream Proposition

I am an Angel
loosed by God
to reshape your life
and touch your understanding
to show, in faith, love is available
  and witness naked truth

  now witness naked truth
in faith, my love is available
to touch, feel, understanding
in this shape for life
caught in Flesh
I am your angel

Intervention

wake up:

this ragged life
was once a gift from God.

how would you rewrap your tattered
Present

Atheist II

God lives

in spite of us

or is it you, or you

responsible
             when in our doubt

God dies

To Fly

how high
is not enough
to feel the face of God
snicker, thinking, Jump, little man
how high

In Church Silence

in church silence
eyes closed
everything that goes on is in my head
questioning
like a shifting dress
after pious sermons saying
all comes from heaven by the spirit
yet every proof of God is in this world
each act of passion visible, physical
all chapters verses writ on molecules
even the devil works in a chemical plant
of politics biology money
if it is all from heaven by the spirit
why can't the world shut up and let me listen
over shuffling shoes creak benches
when everything I think is in my head
waiting
in church silence

In the Spirit of eMail

logon
with God's password

send Satan an eMail:
can you tell which message is from

Heaven?

bounce-back:
no such daemon:

message: must go to hell
don't reply: we are inhuman

servers

Turn Tern Turn

a white tern turns toward sunlight
turning to bronze in late afternoon
wings wheeled like a god got loose in sky
left to drop as a stricken kite limbs crossed
dives into water
then laughing rising on confident upward strokes
the circling tern full turns again
toward sunset
turning to gold
it has been a good life day since dawn
lived free, with even the wind behind him
now
reluctantly
like a small child going upstairs to bed
or an old man wanting a final gesture
before sleep
the ghost tern turns to merge with shadow
as a last call cries good bye
echoing
along blurring shores
that return to night

Wake Speech

I must smell my own fingers:
artificial roses, chemical soap;
so now I guess I am preserved
cleaned up and put on display
but if you say
something really selfish I might sit up
best just shut up
about who deserved
what
and leave me in my fading hope
what little of it lingers
that there is a God who gives a damn
so to speak
evening up what people do or think
contradicting the sham
belief that money oversmooths the squeak
of every hypocritical act
and lack of tact
in final speeches hinges closing
ending my view of each relative sneak
while lamplights sink
on my dreary last supposing
that
they don't ever smell *their* fingers
care where but never how they arrive
or what afterstench lingers
this being so
how do they
know
they're still alive

Vision, Heaven

I will see you in Heaven
and you will see me
 you will sketch against blue backdrop clouds bright angels
 while joyous choirs fill conversation pauses
 as creative will is fulfilled in harmony, colour,
 true pleasures known and captured,
 all earthly hungers
 but the will to draw and sing, being satisfied.
You will see me in Heaven
and I will see you
 I will wander endless pathways through Spring woodlands
 playing ideas of time, space, mathematics
 seeking mushroom symmetry under pale May apples
 wet deer track physics making notes photographs
 that last forever in my mind
 I can stop and show you
I will see you in Heaven
and you will see me
 our paths will cross whenever anyone wishes it:
 while we walk I will think and talk obscure dilemmas
 pure logic matter universal constants
 at the same pace your cloud walkway swirls around us
 and your answering perspectives
 are harmonized with the will of chiming angels
You will see me in Heaven
and I will see you
 though we may arrive on different schedules
 it will not seem like waiting
 impatience long disappeared with unequal visions
 of Earth and Sky
 while for you Heaven is, as it must be, art and music
 for me, the wonder of All is a search for truth.

Free Will

did God
miscalculate
his little gift, free will
to love *to hate* to hate *to love*
evil

Not in Heaven: Twisted Mirror Seven

Because I would not give the words to God
must I haunt grey hills forever in dim twilight
drifting back and forth in ghostly shapeless form
along a muffled creek that knows no sunrise
like a mist that never might escape these valleys,
too far from dawn for birdcall summonses;
do I remain a creature blind in darkness
because my faith could not endure full daylight,
but hid from the bright unspoken truth of God?
Because my faith would not endure full daylight,
must I be blind, a creature kept in darkness
too thick to hear his birdcall summonses
like a mist that traps itself in selfish valleys
of muffled creeks that can admit no sunrise,
drifting back and forth in futile phantom form
may I haunt dun hills forever in grim twilight
because I will not say the words for God?

Who Calls

God lost
was falling out
of touch with someone loved
since childhood - who calls - let's get back
old Friend

A Divine Thought

mortals
form opinion
from tiny perspectives

Gods, on the other hand, just Are
Correct

War Orphans

not watched
by God, not helped
by relatives, unloved.
who gives this definition of
freedom

Paradoxical Prayer

O God
from up so high
my wish seems small foolish
how could such Power stoop to grant
Vision

Dream of the Amateur Angels

In the dusk dream-light
like landing mourning doves blurred white
their wings whirred singing: yes, like you
we are set down here for a purpose too,
our journey goes on past the end of night;

when I asked them why
so many were gathered how far to fly,
they replied: we have different things to do
in another latitude, while you
have a debt to redeem before you die -

Then I sighed and slept
till I dreamed that - my God - of all bird-songs - wept
because of the things - angels left - undone;
was it now too late with the set of sun,
were there promises out that could not be kept?

But His clouded face
turned back from night and returned time's grace:
it was dawn today, bright with warming sun;
now was a chance for some good to get done,
and I woke and smiled too as I took my place

in this work of earth
to which some souls surrender themselves from birth,
become amateur angels, turn right from wrong;
thought is their wings, and love is their song:
how each can lift each, is their weight and worth.

One Grave Stone

I would prefer
my name had worn off any stone
than tell I ended up alone
with grief unshared and love unshown

a better mark
if listed grave by frozen lake
were hid by weeds from those awake
than spell out gifts I did not take

If from my dark
what words admit I dreamed a bit
is covered up in spite of it
did touch one tender spark

you may infer
some warmth was felt for those above
whose lovingkindness thinking of
makes eyes and faces blur

I would prefer
if listed grave by frozen lake
is covered up in spite of it
makes eyes and faces blur

you may infer
what words admit I dreamed a bit
were hid by weeds from those awake
with grief unshared and love unshown

Ice Climbing

 hand grips
melt and shift shape, ice fossils
of twig prints, leaf holes
blur and slip under gloved fingers
clutching the frozen cliff I perceive my life
clings in a climb like this
 I am the lost last snowdrift ice explorer
in my private hell Antarctica,
am the one who climbs alone in absolute cold
up the spin of the end of the world
where all chill winds wind one way sinking
tumbling sleet in blizzards down the lone pole mountain
 so what does it mean and why am I here
with my artificial skin and toes and claws
cutting my world into little chips and crevices
groping my way always upward on slick
and unforgiving surface against forces
older than any lifetime: gravity
 wind inattention
  the fear of a careless gesture
 what will it mean to reach the summit
and why do I long to look down
seeing how all evidence must melt
ledges blurring, the whole cold proof of my being
here
turning
to ambiguous ice fossils
 as if my life my climb were always promised
to be forgotten
should ever true spring come to this my glacier
which I continue to climb

True Death

all dreams
come true to death
doubt monsters moil my grave
hope angels smooth my dust remains
all dreams

Free Will

like wind
(God spoke to me)
free will is treacherous:
uplift downdraft watch your wish my
human

Samara

As punishment my soul was sent
a star seed husked for banishment
in Earth of fertile field and hill
to reach back as the daffodil
blossoms to touch the Firmament

Youth quickened: earth-bound bodies went
to heavens of their own consent;
brief introduction to brief thrill
as Punishment.

Now age: my chastened spirit spent,
I question why this life's extent
is limited: why wit and will
to love and laugh, caress, or kill
is moulded back to earth - Earth meant
as Punishment.

Out of Doors

I had forgotten Whose I was;
I walked Your wood in Spring because -
'twas just a lazy thing to do.
I felt no Plan for me from You,
No Purpose to what this life does.

I strode till gloom past willow fuzz
Ignoring poor-will's Summonses:
"Bec-ome   Your-self" they mocked: 'twas true:
I had forgot.

Escaped from climbing offices'
Self-gratulating emphasis
On who you must impress, those who
Take value from a narrow view:
Ours is a wider World, whose Cause
I had forgot.

Judgement

life is
a sacrament
you must keep it wholly
to your own standards: as your own
true judge

Gilt Dust

Dust like guilt
settles in warehouse
on skids of supplies
puffing
as we lift them heavy in gloved hands:
cardboard covered pasta shreds
boxed wheat from BC
potato flakes in flattened paper sacks
and "hybrid" cartons of miscellaneous stuff.
Seems dirty enough to have been here for months
but most donations ship in under two weeks.
As we pack the container
the rhythm of manual labour settles in:
one picks, a second passes, another places
each box and pail, bag, suitcase, canister;
when we rip back cellophane wrap from cartons, sneezes
seize us each but one at a time
like people getting a joke at different speeds.

Somebody says it's time for break;
weak tea a box of day-old timbits
which really aren't half bad.
Nobody grumbles for food here.
Today we send to ? Zambia? Tanzania?
if we think of the recipients in hunger
guilt like dust
settles on warehouse.
Looking back at the load "that's not half bad" "is it raining?"
above the big bay doorway grey sky brightens;
bronze rifting clouds cast a glow round the container
for one golden instant, a feel of warmth in the breeze
as we each return to the work at different speeds
wandering into the light like motes
gilt dust puffs past swirling
over chattering volunteers
and settles in warehouse
on skids of supplies.

Circle of Reason

because
they can't go home
    they must sleep and beg here

because you beg, sleep here: you can't
        go home

On, Wool Gatherers

Not fluff
for brains, but fluff for nests
that's what science teachers say;
but watching the sparrows hurrying back and forth
outside our classroom window
repeatedly returning
like my eyes over the textbook chapter
dashing left and right unendingly
ignoring the green-June lawn, sun-sputtering sprinklers,
flying up to the eaves:
I think, they want fluff for brains.

Dioecious

without orgasm
the male ash-maple tree
scatters its windblown pollen to the world
and in the distant innocent churchyard
the small pale female flowers wait
setting the seed to sow along the street
without orgasm

without orgasm
the priest prepares his Sunday sermon
to scatter its worldworn wisdom to the wind
and sitting in churchpews
the small pale ears of sinners catch at truth
and some few become his children down the street
without orgasm

Last Toast: in memory of Bob Gottschalk

I thought it was you
in the reddish canoe
bobbing and nodding your head
I had just forgot
then I knew it was not
because I remembered: you're dead

you'd come paddle to see
if who's watching was me
or to ask if my drink had the stuff
when I tilted my head
you replied, yes, I'm dead
but you're worth it, that's reason enough

love the day, you would say
as you paddled away,
because we're both worth it, aware
that before it's too late
I should thank my good fate
for kind friends and a great world to share.

though I thought it was you
in the orange canoe
it was sunset that fooled my poor sight,
but your words still remain
in my addled old brain,
that I'm worth it, right up to the night.

so I'll watch the last rays
of this best of my days
and enjoy the whole view to the end,
then saluting your ghost
with our favourite toast
I'll declare, it was worth it, old friend!

The Gift

  once gifts
are set aside
  like tinsel off our tree
torn paper folded   needles swept
  what's left?

  God's left
the brightest Gift
  like tinsel in His light
more than ourselves   we shine who share
  One Gift

Response

I am not your Answer,
am not Called to be an answer,
am not the Friend you begged your God to send.

From random acts
of clumsy accidental kindness
do not infer Divine Providence.

I have nodded through your fable;
it sounded like all such stories:
lies, slanted truths, some hero-victim tales.

I do not see Angels,
am not sent by them,
do not believe they overhear on high.

It is not generosity to listen,
just idle curiosity;
not kindness to show some slight respect
to one so damaged;
it is not faithfulness to be on time,
the traffic was good today.

I am not the Saint you asked for in your prayer,
just an accidental wanderer
brushing the desert edges of your life;
I do not bring fresh water of conversation,
just arid self-absorption.
I am not your answer.

The Scroll of the Violin

shape with
no reason, grope
past whispering strings, feel
stiff tuning pegs, violin scroll
carved, smooth

There are things in mathematics that are known
as certain to be true
for no reason.

There are sacred things in cultures that are saved
and revered
beyond reason.

A system sufficiently complex,
biosphere, economy, religion, organism
will support a few unneeded flourishes.
This is exactly
as much "waste gift" as that system can afford.
Otherwise it gets
dropped, or the system fails.

This is the means upholding art and leisure.
This sources the excess petals on the rose
and the elaborated scroll of this violin.
Our systems generate it, hopefully.

We live longer than necessary
to reproduce ourselves,
or ensure survival of descendants.
We design food, clothing, houses,
sonnets, minuets,
savouring unnecessary detail
because we enjoy this and
because this planet and civilization
presently allow us.

Imagine one were blind or blindfold
touching a violin for the first or only time.
Imagine feeling close while it's being tuned.
Imagine then stroking the scroll of the violin
while the first pure notes begin.

All of this is unnecessary Entire cultures
have existed without stringed instruments.
Stringed instruments have existed without scrolls.
Humans have rested without music
and some without blindfolds.

Certainly the deaf could appreciate
the varnished curves of the scroll
with sympathetic vibration.

These things are true for no reason.
Entire universes may exist
beyond reason.

life has
no reason, tunes
evolving pegs, turning
truth out without proof flourishing
in joy

Trade-Off Question

It begins with some minor discretion.

Waiting for an elevator in suit and tie
deciding on meeting tactics
don't ask yourself tough questions
such as, who will you be
at the end of this struggle?

It continues as simply as breathing.

Floor lights flash and change;
when a deal demands compromise,
do you stop to think who you'll really be after
that next shift of values, distortion
of priorities, betrayal of friendship?

Now it feeds on itself.

Air moves in the shaft;
is it about getting even,
more powerful, richer, what?
having got even, more powerful,
who will you finally be? don't ask yourself.

Ding. elevator. doors open.

Going up or down, sir?

The Secret

Dogs know the secret, laughing up the driveways
as our bicycle whirs past summer flower gardens
and the rain begins, lightly touching turning spokes
tuning the fenders

Squirrels sometimes know the secret
see their tails flash full in the growing drizzle
as they run and leap, not really for food or shelter,
just chattering nonsense

Still the bike pedals on with your heavy breathing
behind me as I sit on the crossbar seat
holding taped handlebars close to the centre
Bump, Nancy

even the little birds might know the secret
if there were any not hiding from the coming storm
now our bicycle turns homeward
Bump, Nancy, crossing the park-end curb
and onto the sidewalk of rocking rhythm
bump, nancy, bump, nancy, pedals coming faster now

you coast and squeeze the brakes by the house with the windchime
which drips in silence watching plastic windmills
and we count the enormous artificial butterflies
one two three nailed to black wet trunks

if I turn to look at you, with your serious hands
balancing the bicycle, two fingers on each brakelever
would I see you see it too

yes the whole big world is out here for us to smile at
and at each other
sharing
this secret

Late Painting

retouching
the cracked pink flowers in their living room frame
imagine how they want to look in sunlight
maybe shifting a little bit to feel the slightest breeze
as delicately as your hands keep moving
in quick and tiny strokes
as if you were repairing the tracks of time
or a jeweller spring-cleaning your own watch to tell the truth

around you your apartment does not creak
the radiator too is silent
all glass shelved knickknacks know their special places
and also keep quiet: nobody nothing moves
if you shift your feet their nylons do not hiss
on the pale plush carpet

This is not how you wanted it to end,
but this is the way it is, so keep on painting;
get every vein into its perfect place,
let every petal blush as if it lived.
You would rather it were God who was up late working
and that it was you as canvas for his strokes,
but since you cannot be beautiful again
you at least repair as much as you can handle.
Keep the curtains closed.
You want to be finished by morning.

Conversion

con job -
it's church fiction -
no god out there loves us
who'd bring   *such radiance*   to me?
Saviour

Things We Give

We give
toys, ties at Xmas, Valentine hearts,
something carefully shopped for birthdays;

a dull day's effort at work,
benefit of doubt, maybe;
a bus seat to an elderly stranger's cane
or pretty young mother with stroller;

patience at home, making
ends meet, while time flies;
we give our lives to acting out clichés
that others think should make us happy
for some small parts we really like;

in tough times a helping hand
or just any hand to hold on to;
like a child climbing the first slide to ride,
we give encouragement on the down side

of our lives. we give too often without thought
of personal needs or final value
of what we give our selves to.

Like a Tadpole

As I crouched staring
into slime-edge of bog-pond,
quick with fear and curiosity
I saw you peek back from your watery shadow
poking one eye for a tremulous instant
to focus onto alien surfaces
and see how the blinding sunwashed world
of shifting shapes attended you.
You'll creep up into air soon enough I would warn you,
and be longing for moisture the first second you leave it.
Still I
stare deep into bog-slime and darkness, fathoming
what after life
could possibly be to be glimpsed from this one.

At a Safe Distance

childhood

    smirks sweetly from

safe distances:
          moved friends,

strained memories,
          other people's

    children

Failure

Hell is where rivers come
to end in endless
hot and dry
they do not merge in some welcoming sea called Heaven
their trials waterfalls are not resolved
in any universal swell of comfort
their molecules are not returned as rain
but are split to silence
they may not add to any distant thunder
or rumour of cloudburst
not even dust remains

thus the divine destination for mortal failure:
Hell is where rivers come.

Just in Passing

a god passed quickly in the breeze,
and crimsoned falling leaves with ease;
a child might press one in a book
all winter long, and later look
at autumn's broad brush way with trees.

down city streets blew maple keys,
toy helicopters children seize
to fly across the gutter-brook
a god passed quickly.

then winter brought the frosty frieze
down windowpanes a child's eye sees
while instant porridge starts to cook
for breakfast in the breakfast nook
as cold snow piles on memories
a god passed quickly.

Welcome to Toronto

This is as far as you go with me
lace tight your walking-shoes
and reach your cardboard suitcase from the back
step out in quickly ending summer sunlight
thumb shadow gestures touch black highway shoulders
cars pass blank windows
swift taillights rush dust swirls around you
unblinking at the twilight city border.

As you follow them
youth certain strides toward Toronto limits
let the steel signs warn you
three million strangers make a population
of transient friendships
as one could let no silence lapse since Barrie
kept chattering with friendly probing questions
then set you down alone in alien dusk
beside pale rows of long indifferent headlamps
to pass you without looking back
this is the city way of brief acquaintance
no goodbye   this is as far
as you go with me.

Motivation

On a good day
words flow like liquid music on their own
and let me speak to strangers
with fluid images in syllables;
when revision's visions make new versions stronger
I can chant a speech to a napkin
or rhyme a rondeau down it's ragged margin,
and the final rhythm steps out on its own
on a good day;
and then I walk and listen in the wood
to songbirds, or come home to some favourite music
and relax into wondering
if this is how it feels to the opera singer
or that warbling hidden hermit thrush
stirring an auditorium of listeners
or touching one wandering human heart
on a good day

Not Black and White

God prefers pastels
when sketching
in his personal sky
and likes to use subtle brush-stroke complications
illogical wisps of cross-wind decorations
caught in impossible sunset colours

and for the rest of us
just lets us have our pure black-and-white hard images
though clearly preferring cloud-framed messenger blue
or spangled almost-utter-darkness
hinting a universe of touched-up shapes
as if modelled by fuzzy or quantum logic

but in our minds
a simple sky seems enough for an Artist's reach
beyond a darkening hillside hinting of trees
lifting vague whispering leaves to the last of twilight
reminding black and white silhouette watchers
with a gesture of almost rainbow gentleness
gleaming until the sun burns down
and evening comes pierced by blue and twinkling stars
that God uses pastels

Atheist

Behind white shirts and flowered hats we meet
to pray creative help for stricken friends;
their fate we all believe in self-deceit
upon our bent of heaven's will depends.
Denied our rites, unfortunates succumb;
revenge is sweet, a few we overlook?
A righteous man, whose friends are stricken dumb,
is stricken, undefended, from the book?
We cannot so conceive our own import,
and hence our failures prove the lack of god;
to drowning man, a straw is last resort;
religion so to weak, and is this odd?
The atheist exhales a knowing sigh:
who live alone in spirit so must die.

Definition

Who never chastens us for yesterday,
  Who knows we are oppressed by passing time;
  Whose blessing is assurance all sublime,
Who faces start and end without dismay;

Who speaks in simple parables to say
  that those who fall are those who yearn to climb;
  Whose laugh is free, but golden in its chime,
Who turns a duty honour, work to play;

Who, knowing life by loving, dares to die;
  Who feels the wind, and glories in the rain;
    Who comes unknown, and gives to learning friends;
Who marvels birds, and teaches men, may fly;
  Who knows past chance can sometimes come again;
    with Whom each pulse begins, each neuron ends.

Faith

Sleep is an act of faith, wherein the world
  Is trusted to be constant, while the mind
  Leaves fact and drab reality behind
And into balmy vacancy is hurled;

Speech is faith in language: meaning curled
  Within the shell of grammar, hopes to find
  An incubation in a climate kind
Where all its glory fully is unfurled.

An act of faith is trusting, but afraid
  Of laughter, misconceptions, and abuse,
    And hence unknown in humans, but for this:

Who sleep and speak, to wake and hear, are made
  A little faithful, somewhat less obtuse,
    And less afraid of Judas in a kiss.

Lost March 17

irish to Irish, no smile
but would to happiness beguile
returned: green verses in your eyes
writ by 'a nice guy - all disguise'

Winter Leaf

Kitchen window
White wood sill
Stainless steel sink

Stainless steel sink

squat faucet handles long chrome tap
shallow bubbles breathing
rubber fingers plastic saucers
amber circles iron frypan

White wood sill

beaded chaining tarnished keys
red elastic broken
paper tickets flower wooden shoes
plastic timer yellow

Kitchen window

loose wind rattles
neighbour bricks long bare wall
level mortar vertical grooves
shadow angles fading morning

Winter leaf

magic broken sparrow hover
touching watching kitchen window
tumble crumpled instant withered
north wind gusting hard white silence

Paddling

I know you're behind me
I only have to absolutely stop
breath everything
I feel your presence alter the shifting hull

   when I squint my eyes
   the canoe shape shimmers I perch high in the bow
   as a wave slaps hard against the side
   I sense the surge of your stroke
   forceful urging forward
   in a rush toward twilight
   am I safe you're behind me

on this tumbling lake to steady my faltering craft
I kneel alone near the middle crouched for control
I jerk to the pull of my own paddle
as a wave slaps hard against the side
backstroke
bringing the bow round pressing my own destination
must get out beyond darkness

   not navigate night your presence is far too powerful
   I hear your paddle drip in its swift arc forward
   I know phosphorescent whirls chuckle the water
   ghostly marks from your stroke
   as a wave slaps hard against the side
   I dare not turn around to discover
   is anyone there no room you could possibly fit in

I feel your presence
although you came to absolutely stop
breath everything
I leave you behind me

Through his Glasses

Abandoned on his dresser-top
still cocked like his head at their own odd angle
to catch the level light they almost twinkle
casting coma shapes like hourglasses
that mark the sure approach of darkness.
Why they need these to dress him one last time,
when it seems almost a shame to touch them
or give them away
                          pick them up:
he saw through these things
stories
          he read at bedtime
                              poems
he once wrote, love letters
that led to begettings and obligations,
the standard structures he left around us.
Parables were made within these frames,
thought up to confuse or surprise we children
who will not forget to
                    grow up to
                              expect to
are they clean
              there's his tissue
                              just a glance to check them
so that's how he'd see the room one last time:
the radio set for other morning,
a dark suit folded like pyjamas,
the sketch of his boat, portrait of his wife,
and the daub an uncle painted of the river
rounding the bend where the dock was added,
all distorted now
brief images blinked away forever.
Put them in the case. Switch the light. The sun set.
Abruptly the whole room looks black in twilight.

White Gifts

Church white gifts:
Food maker labels tinting
Snow tissue shrouded cylinders
Twelve handfuls grace communion table

Empty crowded kitchen table
White packages glow maker labels:
Christmas grace

Hospital Thanksgiving

pale negligee
four children made
get well greeting card:
scarecrow figures rail fencing
wave yellow corn
thanksgiving blackbirds

thin smile stretched white teeth
grind salt
left breast cyst stitches
she sits up
sheer green film cascading
swing points
hands cup firm blurs
get well greeting card
staring bedside table

four child names
fear sucked nipples aching
cardboard sun straw man
home eating turkey

clench stomache
numb sheet knuckles
ears strain
soft smock shuffles whisper
  ... benign ... benign ... benign
jaws tighten
hot shut eyes

Toronto Ducks

chill rain mist
three ducks down from sky
huddle grey breakwater

call to the ducks
               float closer

brown sand silt streaks black
wet pebbles   glass splinters   concrete chips
red brick edges
rock growing green
slow brown swells blurring jumbled shards

talk to the ducks
               float closer

waves shrug boulder point
pink granite   mortar   dark steel
covered tunnel fingers lake
sewer outlet dark water
dull rainbow oil grey sky

wide culvert mouth
echoing
      ducks
            float closer

rain dropped beaks

Dissection

The scissors are small and sharp steel handles hurt from cutting.

Stab the point through skin and fur, slice ligaments tight forceps
gripping ribs, slide scalpel sharpness under yellow jelly tissues.

The large dull-purple three-lobed organ is the liver: when living

    it converts all simple sugars into glucose
    deaminates excess amino acids
    and stores glycogen

the bright green pebble is the gall bladder: do not rupture it

Formaldehyde stung eyes, nose dripping, squint unwinding grey slick
lengths of small intestine, carve carefully translucent webs of pancreas

    digestive tract from teeth to anus
    sex organs
    bone muscle tendons
    spinal column brain cells nerves
    heart lungs blood vessels red and blue injected plastic
    dead systems tangled still wide eyes

    this is not a rabbit

chewing at clover,
sniffing damp air over morning earth,
crouching in scrub leaves rustled,
claw soft digging darkness

at the edge of a carrot farm mating
under the shadow of split rail fencing some acre

    beyond these boundaries

Road's End

At the bridge the lane confesses
that like all our roads it led to no place;
faint ruts go on left out into a field
down an embankment, past a long hedgerow
where a harvest machine marks the end of its line
and distant men watch us as separate phenomena.

This too is where the river could have led us
if the car were too easy or the walk in too far;
if a kingfisher rattles us passing downstream
it's because he's aware at this end of the world.

Let's just spread our picnic and not get too serious.
Let the reaping device drum its mechanized route
without our attention. Let's just act like friends
on the last day of Summer, at the end of a byway.

Pass the butter; I'll do the bread. You manage the cheese;
I'll open the pop later so leave it in shade;
Is there salt? Yes mustard too for the ham if you like;
No cup. You'll have to drink straight from the can.

If I simply forget our immediate history,
there are clouds shaped like lovers merged far to the west;
there are wildflowers, clover smells, honeybees buzzing of sweetness
and the kingfisher chortling that all of life is now.

Now I help you shake out my last crumbs from your blanket
as a final gesture of acceptance at departure;
pack the food, gather the cans and arrange them
in the very same bags all the garbage should fit
just as our lives would fold back into the same
attitudes exactly if all steps could be retracted.

After Vacation, Homecoming

Tomorrow we sleep late
lift down your suitcase from our bed
worn spread familiar
the wall clock read two thirty
now echoes ticking down the hall
our dust house creaking
we have come back
past torn news papers lawns outgrown
and our clothes need washing.

Eyes rub thumb pressure into skulls
turn down the bed turn down our bodies
tumble facing sleep
we have come back
shrill airplane taxi shuffle feet
long standing luggage eyes lined waiting
dreams now foreign slip between
thin sheets confusing memories
repeat repeat vacation pictures
quick scenes caught bright living cameras
merge continents
in childish leaps of storytelling.

In sleep grey mountains old with snow
confine sky blue deep glacier lakes
streams chanting castle placenames
stoop native costumes halting English lips
grave sign directions
climb rented chariot lurching switchback passes
turn evening shadows hostel houses
night guests touching narrow beds
we haunt in dream.

New sleep apart returning
tomorrow visions reach familiar futures
exploring ordinary places
habitual faces
will rise to breakfast look to find old patterns
from new perspective:
after vacation, homecoming
and one long needed rest
restores us to our selves within ourselves.

Choice

one flower petal

picked for yes, the right answer -

nothing else counted.

www.ingramcontent.com/pod-product-compliance
Lightning Source LLC
Chambersburg PA
CBHW051702090426
42736CB00013B/2500